The Scripture Life at Home

A Resource Book for Applying God's Word to Daily Life

Angie Sommer

Copyright © 2017 by The Scripture Life

All rights reserved. No part of this book may be reproduced or copied in any form without written permission from the publisher, except for brief excerpts in reviews. Requests for permission should be sent to:

Permissions
The Scripture Life
6950 Fulton St.
Houston, TX 77022

www.thescripturelife.com

First Edition

ISBN 978-1-63577-910-3

Scriptures taken from the New King James Version®. Copyright © 1982 by Thomas Nelson. Used by permission. All rights reserved.
Scriptures marked (NLT) are taken from the Holy Bible, New Living Translation, copyright © 1996, 2004, 2007 by Tyndale House Foundation. Used by permission of Tyndale House Publishers, Inc., Carol Stream, Illinois 60188. All rights reserved.

Printed in the United States of America.

Contents

About the Author 5
Chapter 1: The Challenge 7
Chapter 2: The Visible Word of God 13
Chapter 3: Family Devotion Time 23
Chapter 4: Daily Bible Reading 31
Chapter 5: Write It Down! 39
Chapter 6: Make Time for "Us" 47
Chapter 7: Resources 53
Simple Table Scriptures 55
Scriptures by Topic 61
Bible Quiz Questions 105
Bible Board Games 117
Bible Movies/TV Shows 119
Books of the Bible 121
Notes 125

About the Author

Married for over 19 years, Angie Sommer is a proud mom to six children (No, no twins—she gets asked that question a lot!). With a B.S. degree in teaching, she taught kindergarten in public schools, and served as Education Coordinator for Head Start.

When Angie got married, she resigned from teaching. She purposed, alongside her husband, John, to raise a family to be faithful to God, His house, and His Word. Angie and John have been involved in church ministry their whole married life—in Music Minstry (Her husband is keyboard player/band director, and she sings on the Worship Team) and Youth Ministry (Presently, they both direct the Youth Band in which their daughter plays keyboard, one son plays drums, another son plays bass guitar, and another son plays acoustic guitar). Angie loves to lead people in Praise and Worship, and is part of the ladies Bible study leadership team at her church. She is passionate about the Word of God!

After having the privilege of being part of a women's missions trip to Alaska in 2016, God inspired her to create **Scripture Meditation & Prayer Journals** specifically designed to write out Scripture and meditate on what God is saying through His Word. Angie felt prompted to create *The Scripture Life* for the purpose of providing materials to help others live life by the Word of God.

Chapter 1

The Challenge

IT IS WRITTEN,

When my husband and I first married, we shared the way we were raised by our parents. We were both raised by Christian parents, but he was raised in New York and I was raised in the great state of Texas! (I can add that description because I am the one writing this!) There were some differences, but we were both taught to be faithful to God's house, to read His Word, and to live lives patterned after Jesus. These attributes were on my "List of Things I Wanted in a Husband." I wanted to be paired with someone who had the same vision for raising a Christian family: someone who would make church attendance just part of regular life, someone who would lead by example in reading and studying God's Word, and someone who would serve in church with the talents God gave him. God is so good! He gave me exactly what I asked for! We are equally yoked with a purpose of raising our children in the house of God, to serve God, to be witnesses, and to love and live for Jesus!

One of my favorite passages about God's Word is **Deuteronomy 6:4-9**:

> "Hear, O Israel: The Lord our God, the Lord is one! You shall love the Lord your God with all your heart, with all your soul, and with all your strength. And these words which I command you today shall be in your heart. You shall teach them diligently to your children, and shall talk of them when you sit in your house, when you walk by the way, when you lie down, and when you rise up. You shall bind them as a sign on your hand, and they shall be as frontlets between your eyes. You shall write them

on the doorposts of your house and on your gates."

That's a challenge to parents: to teach your children the Word of God, all the time. God commanded the Israelites to teach His Word DILIGENTLY. That means we must be purposeful in it! We must plan in it into our daily lives. Which also means, as moms and dads we better know the Word and still be studying it daily! Our kids will learn more by example than anything else! When you go to the store, soccer field, school, ballet, church, are you talking about God's Word? When you put your kids to bed at night, are you reading or discussing God's Word? When you wake up in the morning, are you reading God's Word? The more we read it and talk about it, the more it will take root down deep into our hearts and souls.

I ask you, is God's Word a priority in your life? Do you take time out of your day to read it? Study it? Do you meditate on it throughout the day? In **Colossians 3:16**, Paul tells us to

> Let the word of Christ dwell in you richly in all wisdom.

In **Psalm 119:11** David states,

> Your word I have hidden in my heart, That I might not sin against You.

And Jesus said in **Luke 4:4**,

"It is written, 'Man shall not live by bread alone, but by every word of God.'"

So are you up for the challenge? Are you ready to start being purposeful and diligent in planning time for reading—studying—meditating on God's Word in your daily life? Are you ready to plan time for the Bible into your family's daily life? If so, this is the book for you! In the remainder of this book you will find practical and tactical ways that my husband and I have implemented God's Word into our family's life. Let's get started!

Chapter 2

The Visible Word of God

IT IS WRITTEN,

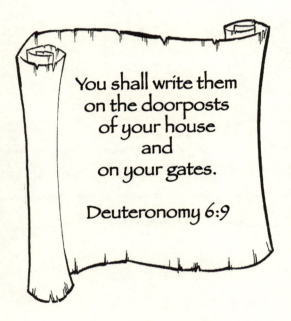

You shall write them on the doorposts of your house and on your gates.

Deuteronomy 6:9

Once we began having children, my husband and I started thinking of ways to teach God's Word to our children. My husband told me that when he was young, his dad would have them quote Scriptures at the dinner table before they ate dinner and then sing a song. I thought the quoting Scriptures at the dinner table was a great way to introduce Scripture to the kids. Since we planned to have dinner as a family every evening, and since you have a captive audience at the table waiting to eat, what better time to quote God's Word? So I began to search up simple Scriptures that the young kids could read and learn. I printed them on parchment paper, using a large font, and placed them on the wall beside the dinner table. I even burned the edges of the paper just to make them look more special. We began allowing our children to take turns each night of the week saying the prayer over our dinner meal. Each night of the week, Monday through Saturday (since we now have six kids), our kids take turns praying over the meal. Sundays, either my husband or I do the praying. With the Scriptures on the wall, whoever is praying gets to choose one Scripture to read, and we all read it together as a family.

When we moved to our new house (because we literally outgrew the first one), I decided to put the printed **Table Scriptures** in frames and hang them on the wall by our dinner table. When we have people over for fellowship and/or dinner, they usually ask about the Scriptures. I gladly share with them our **Table Scripture** family tradition. I was talking with one of my friends who told me she was wanting to implement the framed Scriptures at her dinner table. My friend had just moved into a new house and she wanted to start this tradition in her family. She told me that she just didn't have the time to research what Scriptures to start with, where to find them, or even what topics would be best. My sweet sister-in-Christ is a working mom with three children. She suggested to me that I write a book about different ways to teach God's Word to children in a family setting. I took this as a prompting by the Holy Spirit to use me to help others foster a love of God's Word in their homes and in their families! So here I am writing this book as a resource for moms, dads, or whoever wishes to put Scripture into their daily lives.

When we were building our house over eight years ago, my desire was to place Scripture in every room, and sometimes more than one! I wanted to write God's Word all over the place so that wherever my children looked, they saw it! So, in addition to our Scripture frames at the dinner table, I started looking for either self-adhesive wall Scriptures, framed Scriptures, or Scripture plaques to put in every room. I have slowly added at least one to each room of my home.

For example, in the kitchen or dining room, you might choose a Scripture pertaining to eating or gathering together to give thanks:

- Oh, taste and see that the Lord is good; Blessed is the man who trusts in Him! Psalm 34:8

- in everything give thanks; for this is the will of God in Christ Jesus for you. 1 Thessalonians 5:18

- And Jesus said to them, "I am the bread of life. He

who comes to Me shall never hunger, and he who believes in Me shall never thirst. John 6:35

- for the kingdom of God is not eating and drinking, but righteousness and peace and joy in the Holy Spirit. Romans 14:17

In the study, workroom, laundry room or playroom you can put up some Scriptures about work, studying, or getting along:

- Be diligent to present yourself approved to God, a worker who does not need to be ashamed, rightly dividing the word of truth. 1 Timothy 2:15

- If any of you lacks wisdom, let him ask of God, who gives to all liberally and without reproach, and it will be given to him. James 1:5

- The fear of the Lord is the beginning of wisdom; A good understanding have all those who do His commandments. His praise endures forever. Psalm 111:10

- The fear of the Lord is the beginning of knowledge, But fools despise wisdom and instruction. Proverbs 1:7

- How much better to get wisdom than gold! And to get understanding is to be chosen rather than silver. Proverbs 16:16

- Behold, how good and how pleasant it is For brethren to dwell together in unity! Psalm 133:1

- Let the words of my mouth and the meditation of my heart Be acceptable in Your sight, O Lord, my strength and my Redeemer. Psalm 19:14

- And whatever you do in word or deed, do all in the name of the Lord Jesus, giving thanks to God the Father through Him. Colossians 3:17

- And whatever you do, do it heartily, as to the Lord and not to men. Colossians 3:23

Here are some Scriptures pertaining to what we should be watching and seeking after to place in the living room or media room:

- But as for me and my house, we will serve the Lord. Joshua 24:15(b)

- Abstain from every form of evil. 1 Thessalonians 5:22

- Do not love the world or the things in the world. If anyone loves the world, the love of the Father is not in him. 1 John 2:15

- But seek first the kingdom of God and His righteousness, and all these things shall be added to you. Matthew 6:33

- Finally, brethren, whatever things are true, whatever things are noble, whatever things are just, whatever things are pure, whatever things are lovely, whatever things are of good report, if there is any virtue and if there is anything praiseworthy—meditate on these things. Philippians 4:8

For the bedrooms, you might choose Scriptures about rest, sleep, and not being afraid or fearful:

- I will both lie down in peace, and sleep; For You alone, O Lord, make me dwell in safety. Psalm 4:8

- When you lie down, you will not be afraid; Yes, you will lie down and your sleep will be sweet. Proverbs 3:24

- Come to Me, all you who labor and are heavy laden, and I will give you rest. Matthew 11:28

- He makes me to lie down in green pastures; He leads me beside the still waters. He restores my soul Psalm 23:2-3(a)

- For God has not given us a spirit of fear, but of power and of love and of a sound mind. 2 Timothy 1:7

- "Have I not commanded you? Be strong and of good courage; do not be afraid, nor be dismayed, for the Lord your God is with you wherever you go." Joshua 1:9

- You must not fear them, for the Lord your God Himself fights for you. Deuteronomy 3:22

- In God I have put my trust; I will not be afraid. Psalm 56:11

- The Lord is on my side; I will not fear. Psalm 118:6

- Peace I leave with you, My peace I give to you; not as the world gives do I give to you. Let not your heart be troubled, neither let it be afraid. John 14:27

If you have children who are having difficulties in school, whether it's dealing with other children, being bold in being a witness, or just having difficulty learning various subject matter (math, reading, etc.), there are Scriptures for them all! Search up specific Scriptures to help your child with their specific difficulty. Print them out on small cards, or have them write them out on notecards. You can punch holes in the corners of the cards and attach them with a keyring or book ring (loose-leaf binder ring) to their backpack or to their beltloop. That way the Word of God will be close to them when they need it! You might want to choose (or allow your child to choose) a special keyring or keychain to make this **Scripture Card** pack even more special. Your child can decorate a cover notecard with a design and write or print "Scripture Cards," or "My Sword," or "Super Scriptures," or whatever creative title you or your child come up with! The book rings (or loose-leaf binder rings) and the notecards are available to purchase in various colors at your local office supply store or Walmart.

There are so many ways to put Scriptures up in your house: prints, framed printed Scriptures, self stick wall adhesives, tabletop plaques, hanging them above your child's bed in his or her room. If your child is suffering from nightmares, print out Scriptures on fear and read them to your child. Then have your child read them (if they are able to do so on their own), and then place those printed Scriptures under their mattress. It will be a reminder to your child when he or she wakes up afraid. Frame the Scripture or Scriptures and hang them up on the wall above their beds. Put Scriptures anywhere you think they will see them and read them. **Hebrews 4:12** states,

> For the word of God is living and powerful,
> and sharper than any two-edged sword,
> piercing even to the division of soul and spirit,
> and of joints and marrow, and is a discerner of the
> thoughts and intents of the heart.

Start using the Word of God to fight the enemy who is out to destroy families and our children! Teach your children that they can use Scripture to help them in difficult situations or problems they may face. It is their weapon!

My 17 year old daughter likes to write Scriptures on her bathroom mirror. She chooses ones that encourage her to shine for Jesus at school. (I am so proud of her!) She also tapes pieces of paper or notecards to the wall by the door of her room with Scriptures to remind her of what she feels God is telling her. I think that is a pretty good place. When she leaves or comes into her room, she sees those Scriptures. My daughter already knows the importance of putting the Word of God on the doorposts!!

I encourage you to do your own Scripture search for your family. The Holy Spirit will direct you as to which ones your family needs to focus on each month. Start with just one or two if you want. We try to switch out our Scriptures each month, but if you feel that your kids haven't really grasped those Scriptures yet, keep going! Also, choose what version of the Bible you would like your family to learn. Make sure it is understandable for your younger children.

With the Internet, we have a world of information right at our fingertips…literally! There are so many great resources available when you search "Scriptures for memorization for children." Sometimes, because of the behavior I see in my kids, I choose verses that will help with that particular issue (fighting, jealousy, pride, etc.). Allow the Holy Spirit to direct you. He knows what your family needs. Pray and seek Him for guidance in choose the Scriptures that best suit your family.

Note: At the end of this book, I have included some suggested Scriptures for you to use in the **Resources** section…just to save you some time!

Chapter 3

Family Devotion Time

IT IS WRITTEN,

...and shall talk of them
when you
sit in your house,
when you walk
by the way,
when you lie down,
and when you rise up.

Deuteronomy 6:7

My husband thought it would be good to implement a **Family Devotion Time** in our daily schedule each night of the week, except for Wednesdays and Sundays (because we are at church those nights). We began reading from simplistic Bible storybooks, and then, as the kids got older, we moved into more in-depth devotionals. When you have younger children, choose Bible storybooks with pictures and read with your child/children. Make it a daily habit. We have a video of our daughter (she's our oldest) reading her devotion book to her daddy when she was three years old. My husband started putting the kids to bed when this momma started having so many babies! I needed to attend to the youngest, so Daddy took on putting the older ones to bed. One night, our daughter told him she wanted to read the devotion. So she did! She used her own words, which were actually pretty close to the words on the page (this book had been read a couple of times). She took pride in this and we recorded it! I loved it! She had already trained herself to reading the Bible every night before bed!

Having a regular, consistent **Family Devotion Time** will help your children know the importance of reading God's Word every day. I'm praying that it will continue long after all my baby birds have left my nest. Here are some of the Bible storybooks we have used through the years:

- ***Little Girls Bible Storybook for Mothers and Daughters*** by Carolyn Larsen
- ***Little Girls Bible Storybook for Fathers and Daughters*** by Carolyn Larsen

- ***Little Boys Bible Storybook for Mothers and Sons*** by Carolyn Larsen
- ***Little Boys Bible Storybook for Fathers and Sons*** by Carolyn Larsen
- ***Egermeier's Bible Story Book*** by Elsie Egermeier and Arlene S. Hall (editor)
- ***Little Visits with God*** by Allan Hart Jahsmann and Martin P. Simon
- ***The Bible Story*** by Arthur S. Maxwell (multiple volumes)
- **The International Children's Devotional Bible** by Robert J. Morgan and Natalie Carabetta
- **Standard Bible Storybook** by Carolyn Larsen
- **Bible Stories** by Martin Manser
- **One Year Book of Devotions for Kids** Childrens Bible Hour (3 volumes)
- **One Year Book of Family Devotions** Tyndale House Publishers (3 volumes)
- **The One Year Book of Josh McDowell's Family Devotions: A Daily Devotional for Passing Biblical Values to the Next Generation** by Josh McDowell and Bob Hostetler
- **The One Year Josh McDowell's Youth Devotions** by Bob Hostetler and Josh McDowell (2 volumes)

Sometimes when we are traveling or on vacation, my husband does a **Bible Quiz** with the kids as our family devotion time. This is great because we have five competitive boys—and competition brings out the best in anyone! It compels my kids to know their Bible stories. He will ask a trivia question to the kids and usually he chooses two kids who are close in age so that the question is age appropriate. The questions get harder the older the kids get. You can choose rewards or prizes for this fun way to talk about God's Word. It's a good idea to keep a Bible and a Bible trivia or quiz book or game in the car, so you always have it! (I have included some Bible trivia questions in the "Resources" section of this book to help you get started!)

I discussed making a **Scripture Card** pack with notecards and a keyring (book or loose-leaf binder ring) in the previous chapter. You can make these special **Scripture Card** packs for your family when you go on vacation or when you are just on-the-go driving from place to place, picking up kids, dropping off kids, going to church, etc. You can use the Scriptures that you are using on the wall by your dinner table, or just some Scriptures that you feel your family needs at the time. These can serve as *mobile* or *traveling* **Family Devotions**. Place a **Scripture Card** pack in your family vehicle or in Mom's purse to keep them handy!

Each night of the week, our kids always seem to ask, "What are we doing tonight?" We have tried to plan something to do each night of the week as a family, except for Wednesday night which is church night for us. We try to have a **"Game Night"** at least once a week. What family doesn't enjoy a good board game? Why not play a game focused on the Bible? There are many board games that have created "Bible" versions. (See the **Resources** section at the end of this book for suggestions!)

You can also change up your **Family Devotion Time** by listening to an audio devotional, such as "Adventures in Odyssey" by *Focus on the Family*. We've done this before, which is something very different for kids nowadays since they are so used to seeing so much via media. When you listen to a story, you have to use your imagination to picture the characters and the environment. We usually discuss the topic or issue the characters were facing once the story is over.

Acting out Bible stories during your family devotion time is something fun for everybody! My husband's father loves to do this with our children when he has the opportunity. David and Goliath, Joseph, Noah, Adam and Eve, Ruth, Mary and Joseph, and so on. And yes, even Mom and Dad can join in the acting! The Bible is so full of drama, it really is better than any sitcom, romcom, or drama on TV or at the theater!

Speaking of the theater and movies, there are also some great movies about Bible stories that have been made. Nowadays the Christian movies that are out there by independent film makers are pretty close to the quality of what Hollywood puts out. I encourage you to search out some Bible stories made into movies. This can change up your family devotions from time to time. I have included just a few of the most recent **Bible movies** available in the *"Resources"* section at the end of this book. There are some older movies made about books of the Bible or stories of the Bible that are good as well.

However, if your kids are like mine, TV and movies are an extreme favorite due to our media-driven generation today. Use media sparingly and always keep the Bible as the main source of your family devotion time. Nothing can replace the written word of God. Any time the Bible story is presented changing the true account or deviating from the actual happenings, take the time to show your children the truth in the Word of God. This will teach them to use the Bible as a filter for everything they see and hear on TV or at the theater, or anywhere for that matter. In **Matthew 24:35**, Jesus said,

> "Heaven and earth will pass away,
> but My words will by no means pass away."

Another fun way to teach the Bible to your kids is to have good old-fashioned **"Sword Drills."** Some of you may have never heard of such a thing. Okay. Here's how you conduct a Sword Drill. First of all everyone needs their own Bible. I purchased *The NKJV Early Readers Bible* (Thomas Nelson) for each our kids to use during **Family Devotion Time**. They are kept in the living room in their own special place. Since we are living in America and have the freedom to own as many Bibles we want to, I thought it was a good investment. jmOnce everyone has a Bible in their hand, Mom or Dad calls out a Scripture reference, like "John 3:16." Then the first one to find it stands up and starts reading. That person wins that round. Then that person gets to call out another Scripture. It's another fun way to teach kids (1) how to look up Scripture and (2) to know the books of the Bible.

This year, we have 17, 15, 14, 13, 10 and 9 year olds in the house, and we decided to do something a little different for our **Family Devotion Time.** I'll explain more later...in a couple of chapters. You'll have to keep reading to find out!

Chapter 4

Daily Bible Reading

IT IS WRITTEN,

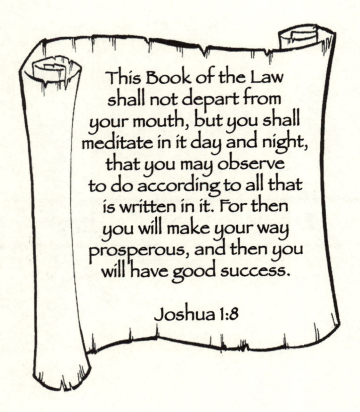

This Book of the Law shall not depart from your mouth, but you shall meditate in it day and night, that you may observe to do according to all that is written in it. For then you will make your way prosperous, and then you will have good success.

Joshua 1:8

When I began having children, I discovered there was not a whole lot of time for me to spend one-on-one with God and His Word. Those babies needed mommy's attention every second of every day. I think it was after I had child number three, I was getting so weary and tired and frustrated that I felt I didn't have time to spend alone with God. After talking about it to my husband, he suggested I get up thirty minutes before I knew baby would wake up and nurse. Now that would be a sacrifice for this sleep-deprived momma! I wanted sleep! But oh was it worth it! I decided to get up around 6:00 am each day, Monday through Friday, to do a Bible study. I needed that time to revive my soul and to give me the extra strength I needed for that day!

We all need it! We need to discipline ourselves to do it. Just like so many people I see posting on Facebook, up before the sun, working out at some fitness place, which is great because we need physical exercise. But we really need our spiritual exercise more than anything! More than food even! Paul tells us in **1 Timothy 4:8** (NLT)

> Physical training is good, but training for godliness is much better, promising benefits in this life and in the life to come.

And isn't knowing Jesus more and more worth the sacrifice? I encourage you to discipline yourself to set aside the same time every day to read, study, and meditate on His Word. And to put into your family's day time to learn Scriptures and study His Word together. Show your kids how to study the Bible. Show them how to pray using Scriptures. Show them how to pray and seek Him for answers to problems and situations that arise in our lives. Show them God is real by doing all those things and watch your kids come to Jesus and give Him their hearts and lives. Praise God!

During one of our church's women's retreats, our pastor's wife challenged all the ladies to read the entire Bible through in one year. This was something that I had really wanted to do all my life. My grandparents had started reading the Bible through together the first year they were married, and have done it every year since! They have been married over seventy years now! That's a whole lot of the Word of God! So I embarked on the challenge myself. I purchased **The One Year® Chronological Bible (NLT)** and started reading, journal in hand! It amazed me that God's Word was so alive and fresh and new! No matter how many times you read it, the Holy Spirit will "highlight" something you have never seen before...something that will change you and work in you through whatever season of life you are in. I have continued to read through the Bible each year since, and it has developed in me a love for the study of His Word.

During the second year I was reading through the Bible, I began to wonder why my kids couldn't do the same. My older ones were definitely reading very long chapter books as required reading in school. Why couldn't they start disciplining themselves to read the entire Bible each year while they were young?

So I began training my children to read the Bible every day. I bought **The One Year® Chronological Bible (NLT)** for everyone 13 years old and older in my family. For my younger boys, I found one-year Bible devotion books with large enough printing for them to read by themselves. Now everyone had a Bible to read at the beginning of each day. My high-schoolers gave me grief because they had to catch the bus for school at 6:10 am. I kept on them, but gave them leniency on the time of day they read their Bible. I told them it didn't matter what time of the day they read, just as long as they read their daily portion of Scripture every day. Pretty soon it became habit in the mornings for my younger ones. They woke up, got dressed, brushed their teeth, came into the kitchen/breakfast area, and grabbed their Bible and started reading. The nice thing about a one-year Bible or devotional is that each reading selection is dated for each day of the year. Yes, I did allow the younger kids to skip Saturdays (family days) and Sundays (church days). But I expected my older kids to make up those days they missed.

Here are some One Year Bibles for young kiddos:

- ***The Beginner's Bible for Toddlers*** by Zondervan (large print for early readers)

- ***A Child's First Bible*** by Kenneth N. Taylor (another great large print for early readers)

- ***The Early Reader's Bible*** by V. Gilbert Beers (another great large print for early readers)

- ***My First Read and Learn Bible*** by Eva Moore and American Bible Society

Some Bibles are available in giant print which is great for young early readers as well. The following Bibles have smaller print than the above, but are the next step in getting closer to reading the Bible in its entirety:

- **My First Study Bible: Exploring God's Word On My Own!** by Paul J. Loth

- **The One-Year® Bible for Kids, Challenge Edition (NLT)** by Tyndale

- **The One-Year® Bible for Kids (NLT)** by Tyndale

- **The One-Year Children's Bible** by Rhona Davies (Tyndale House)

- **The NLT One Year Bible for Children** by V. Gilbert Beers (Tyndale House)

- **Day By Day Kids Bible: The Bible for Young Readers** by Karyn Henley

I recommend you always check the text size if you are looking to purchase online. The larger the text size, the better for those young early readers. Start with Bible Storybooks, just having them read one story a day. The older they get, they can start moving towards reading the whole Bible in one year in its entirety. That should be your goal. I feel it's important for everyone in the family to have a "Bible" to read by themselves in the mornings. Even if you have non-readers, give them Bible storybooks that are mainly pictures. This will not only help them develop the habit, but every time the younger ones finished a "Bible," they felt so proud of themselves! It gives them a sense of accomplishment and will keep them in the Word of God!

This year in January, we started all over again. This time we're reading **The One Year Bible**, not in chronological order, for something different. And I felt that we should all give God the first of our day, so I re-emphasized reading in the morning: before breakfast and before school. It can be done. Don't think that it's too hard a task to have your child read daily from a one year Bible or from a yearly devotional. It just takes discipline. Get those kids up twenty minutes earlier than usual. Start training them now.

There is a trend now to make excuses for not keeping up with Bible reading or devotionals... "Don't beat yourself up if you can't read it every day." "Even if you just read a verse or two, that'll be fine." I'm sorry, but teachers require reading in school and they take NO EXCUSES. Why should God get less than what you are expected to give at school? Our kids will be better if they discipline themselves to read it EVERY DAY! YES... DISCIPLINE! That's not a bad word! Don't we expect our kids to discipline themselves by going to sports practices? Would you let them get by with less time practicing an instrument or half-hearted commitment? Take gymnastics, for example. A gold-medal winner doesn't get the gold because he or she did NOT discipline themselves to practicing EVERY DAY...EVERY WEEK...NO SLACKING. That line of thinking is a strategy of the enemy to keep us moms, dads, and kids alike from reading the Word of God. Why? Because he knows the power of the Word. Jesus used it against him when He was tempted in the wilderness. If Jesus' earthly parents (Mary and Joseph) had decided that it wasn't that important for Jesus to read and memorize Scripture when He was young, how could Jesus have fought the enemy? How do you expect your child to fight against the enemy of his or her soul without the Word of God? How can your child, or even you, know the Word—way down deep within your soul—if he or she or you are not reading—studying—meditating on it?

The Word of God is our Sword (**Ephesians 6:17**), our weapon against the enemy of our souls! The only way to use it effectively is to know it so we can speak it and pray it! The Holy Spirit can't bring Scripture to our minds if we haven't introduced it to our minds by reading it! And we all know reading it isn't enough. We need to write it down, read it again, and meditate on it!

Chapter 5

Write It Down!

IT IS WRITTEN,

Keep my commands
and live,
And my law as the
apple of your eye.
Bind them on
your fingers;
Write them on the
tablet of your heart

Proverbs 7:2-3

In the fall of 2016, I had the privilege of being a part of a women's mission trip to Alaska. We partnered with a local church and conducted their first ever women's conference! WOW! It was amazing to be a part of! Our leader had asked me to lead a workshop titled "Meditation and Prayer." At first, I thought, "I am so unqualified to do this!" Then I felt the Holy Spirit nudging me to take the challenge. Once I began to study what the Word of God said about prayer and meditation, it sparked something in me. I saw the connection between reading the Word of God, writing it down, studying it, meditating on it, and praying it! I wanted to create a journal just for Scripture meditation. I asked my husband, who works in a publishing company, if he thought I could create one in time to send to the ladies who would be attending this women's conference. He said it could be done and then proceeded to instruct me on how to create this journal. By myself! I was a little apprehensive...I had never written anything for publication before. But with God's help, and the direction of my beloved spouse, I did it! We got it done with just enough time to have them shipped to Alaska! And I didn't bring one back with me! There were just enough for all the ladies there! God is good like that, isn't He?

After I returned home to normal "mom" life, I was sharing what God had done in Alaska with some of my sisters-in-Christ at church. I told them all about my **Scripture Meditation & Prayer Journals**. Our youth pastor's wife loved them! She told me it would be great if I had one just for kids. She and her husband had started reading through a book of the Bible at home with their kids for their family devotions. She had just grabbed a regular spiral journal for her kids and was having them write down a verse that meant the most to them from the chapter they read together as a family. One of her kids preferred to draw a picture because it was easier for him to remember the verse that way. Well, that got me thinking, "Why not? Why can't I design a Scripture Journal just for kids?" So, I did! Then I created a Teen version, a version for Men, and a Spanish version (which I am super excited about)! All praise to God! I feel like God is prompting His people to get more into His Word! Dig deeper! Read it more often! Share it with others! And I am thankful that God is giving me the vision to create tools to help others to do just that!

So back to our family devotions. This year we started everyone reading **The One Year® Bible (NLT)** (not Chronological). I gave each member of our family a **Scripture Meditation & Prayer Journal**, and I'm having everyone write down one verse that stood out to them from their daily reading, and then write down what God is saying to them. Then, at the end of the day, we sit down as a family and share which verse we wrote down. I am so excited that my kids are not only learning to read God's Word on their own, in its entirety, but also learning how to apply it specifically to his or her life! I pray as they are reading Scripture and writing it down that it grows deep roots down into their souls. And that they begin really meditating on the words they are reading and writing...and allowing the Holy Spirit to use those powerful Words to change them to be more and more like Jesus, drawing them closer and closer to Him.

Let's get them reading the Word, writing the Word, and hearing the Word! Our job as parents, is to train our children in the ways of the Lord. We can't make them get saved, but we can show them Christ. We can give them the Word of God and discipline them to read it. I tell my kids as much as possible that the Bible, God's Word, is the most important book they need to read. It's more important to read their Bible than it is to do school work, play sports or use/play any media device! It should take precedence over it all!

I know some of you are saying, "I'm not really a 'journal' type person. Why do I have to write it down?" Well I, for one, am thankful that the prophets and the apostles didn't have the same line of thinking. Otherwise, we wouldn't have the physical, tangible Word of God to be able to read! And I'm thankful that godly men risked their lives to translate it into a language my family can understand! All those painstaking hours of writing down word for word so that people of another nations and languages can understand Scripture! Praise God!

Deuteronomy 17:18-20 (NLT) tells us

"When he sits on the throne as king, he must copy for himself this body of instruction on a scroll in the presence of the Levitical priests. He must always keep that copy with him and read it daily as long as he lives. That way he will learn to fear the Lord his God by obeying all the terms of these instructions and decrees. This regular reading will prevent him from becoming proud and acting as if he is above his fellow citizens. It will also prevent him from turning away from these commands in the smallest way."

God expected the ruler of His people to write out His Word and then read it...daily. He was to kept his copy of the Word of God with him at all times. Why? To remind him of God's Law, God's instructions, God's ways. Let me ask you this: How do students learn? By taking notes on the material from a book or from a lecture by the teacher. If a student doesn't write down notes, that student will not learn what he or she is supposed to learn. If we are to be students or disciples of God's Word, we need to read it, write it down, and study it. So let's get those pencils or pens out, and start taking notes on the Word of God! Write down Scripture and then write down what you feel God is trying to tell you!

My hope as a mom is that when my kids leave home, they will continue the discipline of reading—writing—studying—meditating on God's Word. And when they get married and start their own families, the tradition will continue. The Word of God changes lives when it is read, heard, and lived out. Let's keep God's Word as a priority in our homes, in our families, and in our lives. Without it we have no foundation. Jesus said in **Matthew 7:24-25** (NLT)

"Anyone who listens to my teaching and follows it is wise, like a person who builds a house on solid rock. Though the rain comes in torrents and the floodwaters rise and the winds beat against that house, it won't collapse because it is built on bedrock."

His Word is not only the foundation of our homes and families, but it's the centerpiece of the Armor of God, as it is the Truth we wear as a belt around us.

And it is our only weapon as the Sword of the Spirit (**Ephesians 6:14, 17**).

I plan to continue writing materials that will help Christ followers be disciples of His Word. I created "**The Scripture Life**" to provide materials to help others to put the Word of God in every part of our lives... to help us live out Scripture! **Luke 4:4** states,

> But Jesus answered him, saying,
> "It is written, 'Man shall not live by bread alone,
> but by every word of God.'"

If we truly are disciples of Christ, we are students of His Word. And we need to put the Word into practice in each of our lives. **James 1:22** tells us

> "But be doers of the word, and not hearers only"

We can't do what we haven't learned to do. We learn by reading and hearing. We can't read something that hasn't been written. And it all starts at home. We are preparing our children for adulthood, and the best preparation we can give them is the discipline of reading, writing, and knowing God's Word. I want my life to be one that lives out Scripture. I want my kids' lives to be literal, walking Bibles! What better way to show people who God is?

Make your house a house of God's Word, a house of prayer, and a house where the presence of God is felt when anyone walks inside the door. When people come to your house, (electricians or other repair people, neighbors, friends and family) can they tell you are a follower of God's Word? Do they see it on the walls of your home?

Do they hear it being spoken in conversations? Would your life be found GUILTY of being one led by the Word of God?

I found a quote a while back that I really liked, and I actually ended up putting it on a wall in a family gathering room of my home:

> **"Christ is the center of our home,
> a guest at every meal,
> a silent listener to every conversation."**

I hope all who enter my home will know I follow Christ. I hope they see that I am a disciple of His Word, because they can see Scriptures all over the walls and counters and tables in my house. And I pray His presence fills every nook and cranny, as we become more and more a family that prays together, and a family that reads, studies, and meditates on God's Word together! We do our part, and then we allow the Holy Spirit to use the Word that we have deposited within us to change us! After all, God says in **Isaiah 55:11**,

> So shall My word be that goes forth from My mouth; It shall not return to Me void, But it shall accomplish what I please, And it shall prosper in the thing for which I sent it.

Let's get busy doing our part by disciplining ourselves to read, write and study the Word of God, so that He can do His!

Chapter 6

Make Time for "Us"

IT IS WRITTEN,

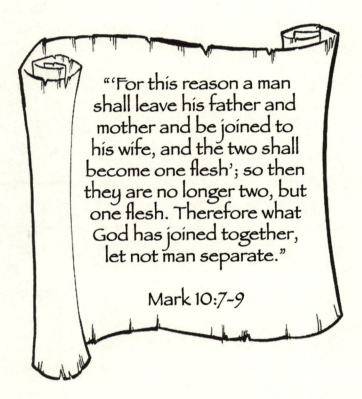

"'For this reason a man shall leave his father and mother and be joined to his wife, and the two shall become one flesh'; so then they are no longer two, but one flesh. Therefore what God has joined together, let not man separate."

Mark 10:7-9

Let's face it. Sometimes our focus can get so child-based that our marriages start to suffer. We love our children, but they can be so needy it seems at times, that the husband and wife relationship is neglected. Moms are sleep deprived with newborns or sick kiddos, or tired because they're having to work away from the home and still have to take care of the home, and dads are tired from dealing with work issues and then coming home to deal with kids' issues (discipline, school, etc.) Family begins with Mom and Dad. Don't neglect time together, especially time together in God's Word. Once the kids go to bed, you two can share your own devotional designed with marriage in mind. Here are some devotionals you can use for just you and your spouse:

- ❤ *Quiet Times For Couples* by H. Norman Wright
- ❤ *Quiet Times For Parents* by H. Norman Wright
- ❤ *Night Light: A Devotional for Couples* by James C. & Shirley Dobson
- ❤ *Moments Together for Couples: 365 Daily Devotions for Drawing Near to God & One Another* by Dennis & Barbara Rainey
- ❤ *Moments with You: Daily Connections for Couples* by Dennis & Barbara Rainey
- ❤ *The Love Dare Day by Day: A Year of Devotions for Couples* by Stephen Kendrick and Alex Kendrick
- ❤ *The One Year Love Talk Devotional for Couples* by Les & Leslie Parrott
- ❤ *Intimate Moments: Daily Devotions for*

Couples by David & Teresa Ferguson, Chris & Holly Thurman

❤ ***The One Year Devotions for Couples: 365 Inspirational Readings***
by David & Teresa Ferguson

The ladies in my church have Bible studies three times a year. This is such an awesome time together in a small group setting, studying Scripture together. During these studies, my husband wants me to get a book for him, so that he can do the study with me. I love that he wants to join me in these studies! I enjoy studying with the ladies, but there's something special about studying the Word of God with my husband. It helps me stay on track and I get to discuss the material with him. It makes our bond to each other stronger and our growth in the Lord deeper.

And don't forget to PRAY TOGETHER! I think the reason Jesus said in **Matthew 18:18-20**

"Assuredly, I say to you, whatever you bind on earth will be bound in heaven, and whatever you loose on earth will be loosed in heaven. Again I say to you that if two of you agree on earth concerning anything that they ask, it will be done for them by My Father in heaven. For where two or three are gathered together in My name, I am there in the midst of them."

is because Jesus knew the power of two was strong. When a husband and wife are in unity and in agreement, they can touch heaven with their prayers!

God created marriage in the beginning, between

one man and one woman. He knew that man and wife together in unity would be powerful in Him! Keep God in the center of your marriage, and in the center of your family! What better way to show your children the example of a successful, blessed marriage. A couple that prays together and reads God's Word together will stay together, keeping the family together in a strong bond. If you keep God in the center of your marriage and the center of your family by using His Word as your foundation, God will bless them both!

Chapter 7

Resources

Simple Table Scriptures

The following forty-eight Scriptures are to help you get started using **Table Scriptures** at your family dining or breakfast table. They are simple Scriptures taken directly from the *New King James Version®* of the Bible.

You can print these Scriptures out individually on 8½ x 11 inch paper, and then cut them down to fit an 8 x 10 sized frame. Design them to fit your own style! You can use a fun patterned or colored paper. Choose a fancy font, an old-style font, or use large print font if you have younger children who are able to read. You can always print these Scriptures out on a larger size paper if you have larger frames that you would like to put them in. Find special frames to use so that your family knows these **Table Scriptures** are special and important. There are many stores that carry unique picture frames. You can even make shopping for the frames a special family outing!

You can start with one framed Scripture if you would like, and then work your way up to four! Or you many only have room for one or two, depending on the wall space by your family table. Just make sure that everyone can see the **Table Scriptures** while sitting at the table, so they will all be able to read them.

- ☐ In the beginning God created the heavens and the earth. Genesis 1:1
- ☐ We love Him because He first loved us. 1 John 4:19
- ☐ Your word is a lamp to my feet And a light to my path. Psalm 119:105
- ☐ I can do all things through Christ who strengthens me. Philippians 4:13
- ☐ The Lord is my shepherd; I shall not want. Psalm 23:1
- ☐ Children, obey your parents in the Lord, for this is right. Ephesians 6:1
- ☐ for all have sinned and fall short of the glory of God. Romans 3:23
- ☐ Jesus Christ is the same yesterday, today, and forever. Hebrews 13:8
- ☐ Oh, give thanks to the Lord, for He is good! For His mercy endures forever. Psalm 136:1
- ☐ Casting all your care upon Him, for He cares for you. 1 Peter 5:7
- ☐ For with God nothing will be impossible. Luke 1:37
- ☐ Pray without ceasing, 1 Thessalonians 5:17
- ☐ For You are my hope, O Lord GOD; You are my trust from my youth. Psalm 71:5
- ☐ Keep your tongue from evil, And your lips from speaking deceit. Psalm 34:13

- ☐ Do all things without complaining and disputing, Philippians 2:14

- ☐ God is our refuge and strength, A very present help in trouble. Psalm 46:1

- ☐ Rejoice in the Lord always. Again I will say, rejoice! Philippians 4:4

- ☐ Whenever I am afraid, I will trust in You. Psalm 56:3

- ☐ Therefore submit to God. Resist the devil and he will flee from you. James 4:7

- ☐ Do to others as you would like them to do to you Luke 6:31

- ☐ Depart from evil and do good; Seek peace and pursue it. Psalm 34:14

- ☐ A soft answer turns away wrath, But a harsh word stirs up anger. Proverbs 15:1

- ☐ Jesus Christ is the same yesterday, today, and forever. Hebrews 13:8

- ☐ For You are great, and do wondrous things; You alone are God. Psalm 86:10

- ☐ This is the day the Lord has made; We will rejoice and be glad in it. Psalm 118:24

- ☐ Do not be overcome by evil, but overcome evil with good. Romans 12:21

- ☐ He gives power to the weak, And to those who have no might He increases strength. Isaiah 40:29

- ☐ In the beginning was the Word, and the Word was with God, and the Word was God. John 1:1

- ☐ Oh, give thanks to the Lord, for He is good! For His mercy endures forever. Psalm 118:1

- ☐ In everything give thanks; for this is the will of God in Christ Jesus for you. 1 Thessalonians 5:18

- ☐ Be kindly affectionate to one another with brotherly love, in honor giving preference to one another; Romans 12:10

- ☐ And whatever you do, do it heartily, as to the Lord and not to men, Colossians 3:23

- ☐ For the Lord Most High is awesome; He is a great King over all the earth. Psalm 47:2

- ☐ Let not your heart be troubled; you believe in God, believe also in Me. John 14:1

- ☐ It is good to give thanks to the Lord, And to sing praises to Your name, O Most High. Psalm 92:1

- ☐ "Ask, and it will be given to you; seek, and you will find; knock, and it will be opened to you. Matthew 7:7

- ☐ Your word I have hidden in my heart, That I might not sin against You. Psalm 119:11

- ☐ If we confess our sins, He is faithful and just to forgive us our sins and to cleanse us from all unrighteousness. 1 John 1:9

- ☐ Trust in the Lord with all your heart, And lean not on your own understanding, Proverbs 3:5

- ☐ And whatever things you ask in prayer, believing, you will receive. Matthew 21:22

- ☐ For God so loved the world that He gave His only begotten Son, that whoever believes in Him should not perish but have everlasting life. John 3:16

- ☐ You shall love the Lord your God with all your heart, with all your soul, and with all your strength. Deuteronomy 6:5

- ☐ And be kind to one another, tenderhearted, forgiving one another, even as God in Christ forgave you. Ephesians 4:32

- ☐ And my God shall supply all your need according to His riches in glory by Christ Jesus. Philippians 4:19

- ☐ Let the words of my mouth and the meditation of my heart, Be acceptable in Your sight, O Lord, my strength and my Redeemer. Psalm 19:14

- ☐ Beloved, let us love one another, for love is of God; and everyone who loves is born of God and knows God. 1 John 4:7

- ☐ I will praise You, for I am fearfully and wonderfully made; Marvelous are Your works, And that my soul knows very well. Psalm 139:14

- ☐ Let your light so shine before men, that they may see your good works and glorify your Father in heaven. Matthew 5:16

Scriptures by Topic

The following is a list of Scriptures on various topics that I felt would benefit you as a family. I have also included scriptures pertaining to certain holidays. All scriptures are listed in the *New King James Version®*, unless otherwise noted. Some of the topics are related to holidays and seasons. Feel free to use another Bible version of any of the verses that are listed. I encourage you to be led by the Holy Spirit in choosing Scriptures for your family to learn. The Bible is full of wisdom for all areas of life. You might even want your older children to research Scriptures that deal with a specific topic that they are interested in, or a topic that they need to know what God's Word says about it. Have them use the Concordance at the back of their Bible, or **Strong's Exhaustive Concordance of the Bible** by James Strong. There are also many websites where you can search Scriptures by topic. Here are few:

- www.biblegateway.com
- www.biblestudytools.com
- www.blueletterbible.org
- www.bible.org

Christmas

- For unto us a Child is born, Unto us a Son is given; And the government will be upon His shoulder. And His name will be called Wonderful, Counselor, Mighty God, Everlasting Father, Prince of Peace. Isaiah 9:6

- And she will bring forth a Son, and you shall call His name Jesus, for He will save His people from their sins. Matthew 1:21

- "Behold, the virgin shall be with child, and bear a Son, and they shall call His name Immanuel," which is translated, "God with us." Matthew 1:23

- And when they had come into the house, they saw the young Child with Mary His mother, and fell down and worshiped Him. And when they had opened their treasures, they presented gifts to Him: gold, frankincense, and myrrh. Matthew 2:11

- And the angel answered and said to her, "The Holy Spirit will come upon you, and the power of the Highest will overshadow you; therefore, also, that Holy One who is to be born will be called the Son of God. Luke 1:35

- For there is born to you this day in the city of David a Savior, who is Christ the Lord. Luke 2:11

- Then the angel said to her, "Do not be afraid, Mary, for you have found favor with God. And behold, you will conceive in your womb and bring forth a Son, and shall call His name Jesus. He will be great, and will be called the Son of the Highest; and the Lord God will give Him the throne of His father David. Luke 1:30-32

- And the angel answered and said to her, "The Holy Spirit will come upon you, and the power of the Highest will overshadow you; therefore, also, that Holy One who is to be born will be called the Son of God. Luke 1:35

- And she brought forth her firstborn Son, and wrapped Him in swaddling cloths, and laid Him in a manger, because there was no room for them in the inn. Luke 2:7

- Then the angel said to them, "Do not be afraid, for behold, I bring you good tidings of great joy which will be to all people. For there is born to you this day in the city of David a Savior, who is Christ the Lord. And this will be the sign to you: You will find a Babe wrapped in swaddling cloths, lying in a manger." Luke 2:10-12

Easter/Resurrection

- But the angel answered and said to the women, "Do not be afraid, for I know that you seek Jesus who was crucified. He is not here; for He is risen, as He said. Come, see the place where the Lord lay. Matthew 28:5-6

- But he said to them, "Do not be alarmed. You seek Jesus of Nazareth, who was crucified. He is risen! He is not here. See the place where they laid Him. Mark 16:6

- He is not here, but is risen! Remember how He spoke to you when He was still in Galilee, Luke 24:6

- Jesus said to her, "I am the resurrection and the life. He who believes in Me, though he may die, he shall live. John 11:25

- Knowing that Christ, having been raised from the dead, dies no more. Death no longer has dominion over Him. Romans 6:9

- Who is he who condemns? It is Christ who died, and furthermore is also risen, who is even at the right hand of God, who also makes intercession for us. Romans 8:34

- For I delivered to you first of all that which I also received: that Christ died for our sins according to the Scriptures, and that He was buried, and that He rose again the third day according to the Scriptures, 1 Corinthians 15:3-4

- But now Christ is risen from the dead, and has become the firstfruits of those who have fallen asleep. 1 Corinthians 15:20

- Blessed be the God and Father of our Lord Jesus Christ, who according to His abundant mercy has begotten us again to a living hope through the resurrection of Jesus Christ from the dead, 1 Peter 1:3

- I am He who lives, and was dead, and behold, I am alive forevermore. Amen. And I have the keys of Hades and of Death. Revelation 1:18

Faith

- So the Lord said, "If you have faith as a mustard seed, you can say to this mulberry tree, 'Be pulled up by the roots and be planted in the sea,' and it would obey you. Luke 17:6

- So then faith comes by hearing, and hearing by the word of God. Romans 10:17

- Now faith is the substance of things hoped for, the evidence of things not seen. Hebrews 11:1

- But without faith it is impossible to please Him, for he who comes to God must believe that He is, and that He is a rewarder of those who diligently seek Him. Hebrews 11:6

- Teach me good judgment and knowledge, For I believe Your commandments. Psalm 119:66

- Jesus said to him, "If you can believe, all things are possible to him who believes." Mark 9:23

- For assuredly, I say to you, whoever says to this mountain, 'Be removed and be cast into the sea,' and does not doubt in his heart, but believes that those things he says will be done, he will have whatever he says. Mark 11:23

- Therefore I say to you, whatever things you ask when you pray, believe that you receive them, and you will have them. Mark 11:24

- He who believes and is baptized will be saved; but he who does not believe will be condemned. Mark 16:16

- But as many as received Him, to them He gave the right to become children of God, to those who believe in His name: John 1:12

- For God so loved the world that He gave His only begotten Son, that whoever believes in Him should not perish but have everlasting life. John 3:16

- Jesus said to her, "I am the resurrection and the life. He who believes in Me, though he may die, he shall live. John 11:25

- but these are written that you may believe that Jesus is the Christ, the Son of God, and that believing you may have life in His name. John 20:31

- So they said, "Believe on the Lord Jesus Christ, and you will be saved, you and your household." Acts 16:31

- that if you confess with your mouth the Lord Jesus and believe in your heart that God has raised Him from the dead, you will be saved. Romans 10:9

- Who is he who overcomes the world, but he who believes that Jesus is the Son of God? 1 John 5:5

- These things I have written to you who believe in the name of the Son of God, that you may know that you have eternal life, and that you may continue to believe in the name of the Son of God. 1 John 5:13

Fear

- Have I not commanded you? Be strong and of good courage; do not be afraid, nor be dismayed, for the Lord your God is with you wherever you go." Joshua 1:9

- In God (I will praise His word), In God I have put my trust; I will not fear. What can flesh do to me? Psalm 56:4

- The Lord is on my side; I will not fear. What can man do to me? Psalm 118:6

- Fear not, for I am with you; Be not dismayed, for I am your God. I will strengthen you, Yes, I will help you, I will uphold you with My righteous right hand.' Isaiah 41:10

- For I, the Lord your God, will hold your right hand, Saying to you, 'Fear not, I will help you.' Isaiah 41:13

- Do not fear therefore; you are of more value than many sparrows. Matthew 10:31

- But the very hairs of your head are all numbered. Do not fear therefore; you are of more value than many sparrows. Luke 12:7

- For God has not given us a spirit of fear, but of power and of love and of a sound mind. 2 Timothy 1:7

- There is no fear in love; but perfect love casts out fear, because fear involves torment. But he who fears has not been made perfect in love. 1 John 4:18

Joy

- You will show me the path of life; In Your presence is fullness of joy; At Your right hand are pleasures forevermore. Psalm 16:11

- For His anger is but for a moment, His favor is for life; Weeping may endure for a night, But joy comes in the morning. Psalm 30:5

- Be glad in the Lord and rejoice, you righteous; And shout for joy, all you upright in heart! Psalm 32:11

- And my soul shall be joyful in the Lord; It shall rejoice in His salvation. Psalm 35:9

- Restore to me the joy of Your salvation, And uphold me by Your generous Spirit. Psalm 51:12

- My soul shall be satisfied as with marrow and fatness, And my mouth shall praise You with joyful lips. Psalm 63:5

- Make a joyful shout to God, all the earth! Psalm 66:1

- Oh, let the nations be glad and sing for joy! For You shall judge the people righteously, And govern the nations on earth. Psalm 67:4

- Oh come, let us sing to the Lord! Let us shout joyfully to the Rock of our salvation. Psalm 95:1

- Let us come before His presence with thanksgiving; Let us shout joyfully to Him with psalms. Psalm 95:2

- Shout joyfully to the Lord, all the earth; Break forth in song, rejoice, and sing praises. Psalm 98:4

- With trumpets and the sound of a horn; Shout joyfully before the Lord, the King. Psalm 98:6

- Make a joyful shout to the Lord, all you lands! Psalm 100:1

- He brought out His people with joy, His chosen ones with gladness. Psalm 105:43

- Those who sow in tears Shall reap in joy. Psalm 126:5

- Let Your priests be clothed with righteousness, And let Your saints shout for joy. Psalm 132:9

- Let the saints be joyful in glory; Let them sing aloud on their beds. Psalm 149:5

- Deceit is in the heart of those who devise evil, But counselors of peace have joy. Proverbs 12:20

- It is a joy for the just to do justice, But destruction will come to the workers of iniquity. Proverbs 21:15

- Therefore with joy you will draw water from the wells of salvation. Isaiah 13:3

- And the ransomed of the Lord shall return, And come to Zion with singing, With everlasting joy on their heads. They shall obtain joy and gladness, And sorrow and sighing shall flee away.
Isaiah 35:10

- I will greatly rejoice in the Lord, My soul shall be joyful in my God; For He has clothed me with the garments of salvation, He has covered me with the robe of righteousness, As a bridegroom decks himself with ornaments, And as a bride adorns herself with her jewels. Isaiah 61:10

- Yet I will rejoice in the Lord, I will joy in the God of my salvation. Habakkuk 3:18

- His lord said to him, 'Well done, good and faithful servant; you have been faithful over a few things, I will make you ruler over many things. Enter into the joy of your lord.' Matthew 25:23

- "These things I have spoken to you, that My joy may remain in you, and that your joy may be full.
John 15:11

- Until now you have asked nothing in My name. Ask, and you will receive, that your joy may be full. John 16:24

- 'You have made known to me the ways of life; You will make me full of joy in Your presence.' Acts 2:28

- for the kingdom of God is not eating and drinking, but righteousness and peace and joy in the Holy Spirit. Romans 14:17

- Now may the God of hope fill you with all joy and peace in believing, that you may abound in hope by the power of the Holy Spirit. Romans 15:13

- But the fruit of the Spirit is love, joy, peace, longsuffering, kindness, goodness, faithfulness, gentleness, self-control. Against such there is no law. Galatians 5:22-23

- My brethren, count it all joy when you fall into various trials, James 1:2

- And these things we write to you that your joy may be full. 1 John 1:4

Love

- You shall love the Lord your God with all your heart, with all your soul, and with all your strength. Deuteronomy 6:5

- 'And it shall be that if you earnestly obey My commandments which I command you today, to love the Lord your God and serve Him with all your heart and with all your soul, Deuteronomy 11:13

- "For if you carefully keep all these commandments which I command you to do—to love the Lord your God, to walk in all His ways, and to hold fast to Him— Deuteronomy 11:22

- So be very careful to love the Lord your God. Joshua 23:11 (NLT)

- I will love You, O Lord, my strength. Psalm 18:1

- Oh, how I love Your law! It is my meditation all the day. Psalm 119:97

- Therefore I love Your commandments More than gold, yes, than fine gold! Psalm 119:127

- Hatred stirs up strife, But love covers all sins. Proverbs 10:12

- A friend loves at all times, And a brother is born for adversity. Proverbs 17:17

- But I say to you, love your enemies, bless those who curse you, do good to those who hate you, and pray for those who spitefully use you and persecute you, Matthew 5:44

- Jesus said to him, "'You shall love the Lord your God with all your heart, with all your soul, and with all your mind.' Matthew 22:37

- "But I say to you who hear: Love your enemies, do good to those who hate you, Luke 6:27

- But love your enemies, do good, and lend, hoping for nothing in return; and your reward will be great, and you will be sons of the Most High. For He is kind to the unthankful and evil. Luke 6:35

- A new commandment I give to you, that you love one another; as I have loved you, that you also love one another. John 13:34

- By this all will know that you are My disciples, if you have love for one another." John 13:35

- If you love Me, keep My commandments. John 14:15

- He who has My commandments and keeps them, it is he who loves Me. And he who loves Me will be loved by My Father, and I will love him and manifest Myself to him." John 14:21

- Jesus answered and said to him, "If anyone loves Me, he will keep My word; and My Father will love him, and We will come to him and make Our home with him. John 14:23

- This is My commandment, that you love one another as I have loved you. John 15:12

- Greater love has no one than this, than to lay down one's life for his friends. John 15:13

- Don't just pretend to love others. Really love them. Hate what is wrong. Hold tightly to what is good. Romans 12:9 (NLT)

- Be kindly affectionate to one another with brotherly love, in honor giving preference to one another; Romans 12:10

- Love does no harm to a neighbor; therefore love is the fulfillment of the law. Romans 13:10

- Love suffers long and is kind; love does not envy; love does not parade itself, is not puffed up; 1 Corinthians 13:4

- And now abide faith, hope, love, these three; but the greatest of these is love. 1 Corinthians 13:13

- Let all that you do be done with love. 1 Corinthians 16:14

- For all the law is fulfilled in one word, even in this: "You shall love your neighbor as yourself."
Galatians 5:14

- And walk in love, as Christ also has loved us and given Himself for us, an offering and a sacrifice to God for a sweet-smelling aroma.
Ephesians 5:2

- But above all these things put on love, which is the bond of perfection. Colossians 3:14

- Let no one despise your youth, but be an example to the believers in word, in conduct, in love, in spirit, in faith, in purity. 1 Timothy 4:12

- For God has not given us a spirit of fear, but of power and of love and of a sound mind.
2 Timothy 1:7

- Honor all people. Love the brotherhood. Fear God. Honor the king. 1 Peter 2:17

- Finally, all of you be of one mind, having compassion for one another; love as brothers, be tenderhearted, be courteous; 1 Peter 3:8

- And above all things have fervent love for one another, for "love will cover a multitude of sins."
1 Peter 4:8

- Beloved, let us love one another, for love is of God; and everyone who loves is born of God and knows God. 1 John 4:7

- Beloved, if God so loved us, we also ought to love one another. 1 John 4:11

- No one has seen God at any time. If we love one another, God abides in us, and His love has been perfected in us. 1 John 4:12

- We love Him because He first loved us. 1 John 4:19

- If someone says, "I love God," and hates his brother, he is a liar; for he who does not love his brother whom he has seen, how can he love God whom he has not seen? 1 John 4:20

- And this commandment we have from Him: that he who loves God must love his brother also. 1 John 4:21

- By this we know that we love the children of God, when we love God and keep His commandments. 1 John 5:2

Mind/Thoughts

- Oh, let the wickedness of the wicked come to an end, But establish the just; For the righteous God tests the hearts and minds. Psalm 7:9

- The Lord knows the thoughts of man, That they are futile. Psalm 94:11

- The thoughts of the righteous are right, But the counsels of the wicked are deceitful. Proverbs 12:5

- Commit your works to the Lord, And your thoughts will be established. Proverbs 16:3

- For as he thinks in his heart, so is he. "Eat and drink!" he says to you, But his heart is not with you. Proverbs 23:7

- You will keep him in perfect peace, Whose mind is stayed on You, Because he trusts in You. Isaiah 26:3

- Let none of you think evil in your heart against your neighbor; And do not love a false oath. For all these are things that I hate,' Says the Lord." Zechariah 8:17

- Jesus said to him, "'You shall love the Lord your God with all your heart, with all your soul, and with all your mind.' Matthew 22:37

- "And do not seek what you should eat or what you should drink, nor have an anxious mind. Luke 12:29

- For those who live according to the flesh set their minds on the things of the flesh, but those who live according to the Spirit, the things of the Spirit. Romans 8:5

- For to be carnally minded is death, but to be spiritually minded is life and peace. Romans 8:6

- Because the carnal mind is enmity against God; for it is not subject to the law of God, nor indeed can be. Romans 8:7

- For I say, through the grace given to me, to everyone who is among you, not to think of himself more highly than he ought to think, but to think soberly, as God has dealt to each one a measure of faith. Romans 12:3

- And do not be conformed to this world, but be transformed by the renewing of your mind, that you may prove what is that good and acceptable and perfect will of God. Romans 12:12

- Be of the same mind toward one another. Do not set your mind on high things, but associate with the humble. Do not be wise in your own opinion. Romans 12:16

- Now may the God of patience and comfort grant you to be like-minded toward one another, according to Christ Jesus, Romans 15:9

- that you may with one mind and one mouth glorify the God and Father of our Lord Jesus Christ. Romans 15:6

- Now I plead with you, brethren, by the name of our Lord Jesus Christ, that you all speak the same thing, and that there be no divisions among you, but that you be perfectly joined together in the same mind and in the same judgment. 1 Corinthians 1:10

- For "who has known the mind of the Lord that he may instruct Him?" But we have the mind of Christ. 1 Corinthians 2:16

- And if anyone thinks that he knows anything, he knows nothing yet as he ought to know. 1 Corinthians 8:2

- Therefore let him who thinks he stands take heed lest he fall. 1 Corinthians 10:12

- (Love) does not behave rudely, does not seek its own, is not provoked, thinks no evil; 1 Corinthians 13:5

- Finally, brethren, farewell. Become complete. Be of good comfort, be of one mind, live in peace; and the God of love and peace will be with you. 2 Corinthians 13:11

- For if anyone thinks himself to be something, when he is nothing, he deceives himself. Galatians 6:3

- and be renewed in the spirit of your mind, Ephesians 4:23

- fulfill my joy by being like-minded, having the same love, being of one accord, of one mind. Philippians 2:2

- Let nothing be done through selfish ambition or conceit, but in lowliness of mind let each esteem others better than himself. Philippians 2:3

- Let this mind be in you which was also in Christ Jesus, Philippians 2:5

- and the peace of God, which surpasses all understanding, will guard your hearts and minds through Christ Jesus. Philippians 4:7

- Set your mind on things above, not on things on the earth. Colossians 3:2

- For God has not given us a spirit of fear, but of power and of love and of a sound mind. 2 Timothy 1:7

- If anyone among you thinks he is religious, and does not bridle his tongue but deceives his own heart, this one's religion is useless. James 1:26

- Finally, all of you be of one mind, having compassion for one another; love as brothers, be tenderhearted, be courteous; 1 Peter 3:8

Newness/New Year

- Therefore we were buried with Him through baptism into death, that just as Christ was raised from the dead by the glory of the Father, even so we also should walk in newness of life. Romans 6:4

- But now we have been delivered from the law, having died to what we were held by, so that we should serve in the newness of the Spirit and not in the oldness of the letter. Romans 7:6

- Therefore, if anyone is in Christ, he is a new creation; old things have passed away; behold, all things have become new. 2 Corinthians 5:17

- For in Christ Jesus neither circumcision nor uncircumcision avails anything, but a new creation. Galatians 6:15

- having abolished in His flesh the enmity, that is, the law of commandments contained in ordinances, so as to create in Himself one new man from the two, thus making peace. Ephesians 2:15

- and that you put on the new man which was created according to God, in true righteousness and holiness. Ephesians 4:24

♦ and have put on the new man who is renewed in knowledge according to the image of Him who created him, Colossians 3:10

♦ Then He who sat on the throne said, "Behold, I make all things new." And He said to me, "Write, for these words are true and faithful." Revelation 21:5

Peace

- The Lord will give strength to His people; The Lord will bless His people with peace. Psalm 29:11

- Depart from evil and do good; Seek peace and pursue it. Psalm 34:14

- Mark the blameless man, and observe the upright; For the future of that man is peace. Psalm 37:37

- Great peace have those who love Your law, And nothing causes them to stumble. Psalm 119:165

- You will keep him in perfect peace, Whose mind is stayed on You, Because he trusts in You. Isaiah 26:3

- The work of righteousness will be peace, And the effect of righteousness, quietness and assurance forever. Isaiah 32:7

- My people will dwell in a peaceful habitation, In secure dwellings, and in quiet resting places, Isaiah 32:18

- For I know the thoughts that I think toward you, says the Lord, thoughts of peace and not of evil, to give you a future and a hope. Jeremiah 29:11

- Blessed are the peacemakers, For they shall be called sons of God. Matthew 5:9

- To give light to those who sit in darkness and the shadow of death, To guide our feet into the way of peace." Luke 1:79

- Peace I leave with you, My peace I give to you; not as the world gives do I give to you. Let not your heart be troubled, neither let it be afraid. John 14:27

- These things I have spoken to you, that in Me you may have peace. In the world you will have tribulation; but be of good cheer, I have overcome the world." John 16:33

- Therefore, having been justified by faith, we have peace with God through our Lord Jesus Christ, Romans 5:1 9

- For to be carnally minded is death, but to be spiritually minded is life and peace. Romans 8:6

- If it is possible, as much as depends on you, live peaceably with all men. Romans 12:18

- for the kingdom of God is not eating and drinking, but righteousness and peace and joy in the Holy Spirit. Romans 14:17

- Therefore let us pursue the things which make for peace and the things by which one may edify another. Romans 14:19

- For God is not the author of confusion but of peace, as in all the churches of the saints.
1 Corinthians 14:33

- Finally, brethren, farewell. Become complete. Be of good comfort, be of one mind, live in peace; and the God of love and peace will be with you.
2 Corinthians 13:11

- But the fruit of the Spirit is love, joy, peace, longsuffering, kindness, goodness, faithfulness, gentleness, self-control. Against such there is no law. Galatians 5:22-23

- endeavoring to keep the unity of the Spirit in the bond of peace. Ephesians 4:3

- and having shod your feet with the preparation of the gospel of peace; Ephesians 6:15

- and the peace of God, which surpasses all understanding, will guard your hearts and minds through Christ Jesus. Philippians 4:7

- And let the peace of God rule in your hearts, to which also you were called in one body; and be thankful. Colossians 3:15

- Now may the Lord of peace Himself give you peace always in every way. The Lord be with you all. 2 Thessalonians 3:16

- Flee also youthful lusts; but pursue righteousness, faith, love, peace with those who call on the Lord out of a pure heart. 2 Timothy 2:22

- to speak evil of no one, to be peaceable, gentle, showing all humility to all men. Titus 3:2

- Pursue peace with all people, and holiness, without which no one will see the Lord: Hebrews 12:14

- But the wisdom from above is first of all pure. It is also peace loving, gentle at all times, and willing to yield to others. It is full of mercy and the fruit of good deeds. It shows no favoritism and is always sincere. James 3:17 (NLT)

- Now the fruit of righteousness is sown in peace by those who make peace. James 3:18

- Let him turn away from evil and do good; Let him seek peace and pursue it. 1 Peter 3:11

Strength

- The God of my strength, in whom I will trust; My shield and the horn of my salvation, My stronghold and my refuge; My Savior, You save me from violence. 2 Samuel 22:3

- God is my strength and power, And He makes my way perfect. 2 Samuel 22:33

- For You have armed me with strength for the battle; You have subdued under me those who rose against me. 2 Samuel 22:40

- Seek the Lord and His strength; Seek His face evermore! 1 Chronicles 16:11

- Both riches and honor come from You, And You reign over all. In Your hand is power and might; In Your hand it is to make great And to give strength to all. 1 Chronicles 29:12

- "With Him are wisdom and strength, He has counsel and understanding. Job 12:13

- I will love You, O Lord, my strength. Psalm 18:1

- The Lord is my rock and my fortress and my deliverer; My God, my strength, in whom I will trust; My shield and the horn of my salvation, my stronghold. Psalm 18:2

- It is God who arms me with strength, And makes my way perfect. Psalm 18:32

- For You have armed me with strength for the battle; You have subdued under me those who rose up against me. Psalm 18:39

- Let the words of my mouth and the meditation of my heart Be acceptable in Your sight, O Lord, my strength and my Redeemer. Psalm 19:14

- But You, O Lord, do not be far from Me; O My Strength, hasten to help Me! Psalm 22:19

- Wait on the Lord; Be of good courage, And He shall strengthen your heart; Wait, I say, on the Lord! Psalm 27:4

- The Lord is my strength and my shield; My heart trusted in Him, and I am helped; Therefore my heart greatly rejoices, And with my song I will praise Him. Psalm 28:7

- The Lord is their strength, And He is the saving refuge of His anointed. Psalm 28:8

- The Lord will give strength to His people; The Lord will bless His people with peace. Psalm 29:11

- Be of good courage, And He shall strengthen your heart, All you who hope in the Lord. Psalm 31:24

- But the salvation of the righteous is from the Lord; He is their strength in the time of trouble. Psalm 37:39

- God is our refuge and strength, A very present help in trouble. Psalm 46:1

- I will wait for You, O You his Strength; For God is my defense. Psalm 59:9

- To You, O my Strength, I will sing praises; For God is my defense, My God of mercy. Psalm 59:17

- In God is my salvation and my glory; The rock of my strength, And my refuge, is in God. Psalm 62:7

- O God, You are more awesome than Your holy places. The God of Israel is He who gives strength and power to His people. Blessed be God! Psalm 68:35

- I will go in the strength of the Lord GOD; I will make mention of Your righteousness, of Yours only. Psalm 71:16

- My flesh and my heart fail; But God is the strength of my heart and my portion forever. Psalm 73:26

- Seek the Lord and His strength; Seek His face evermore! Psalm 105:4

- The Lord is my strength and song, And He has become my salvation. Psalm 118:14

- O GOD the Lord, the strength of my salvation, You have covered my head in the day of battle. Psalm 140:7

- The way of the Lord is strength for the upright, But destruction will come to the workers of iniquity. Proverbs 10:29

- The name of the Lord is a strong tower; The righteous run to it and are safe. Proverbs 18:10

- Behold, God is my salvation, I will trust and not be afraid; 'For YAH, the Lord, is my strength and song; He also has become my salvation.'" Isaiah 12:2

- Trust in the Lord forever, For in YAH, the Lord, is everlasting strength. Isaiah 26:4

- He gives power to the weak, And to those who have no might He increases strength. Isaiah 40:29

- But those who wait on the Lord Shall renew their strength; They shall mount up with wings like eagles, They shall run and not be weary, They shall walk and not faint. Isaiah 40:31

- Fear not, for I am with you; Be not dismayed, for I am your God. I will strengthen you, Yes, I will help you, I will uphold you with My righteous right hand.' Isaiah 41:10

- The Lord God is my strength; He will make my feet like deer's feet, And He will make me walk on my high hills. Habakkuk 3:19

- And you shall love the Lord your God with all your heart, with all your soul, with all your mind, and with all your strength.' This is the first commandment. Mark 12:30

- And He said to me, "My grace is sufficient for you, for My strength is made perfect in weakness." Therefore most gladly I will rather boast in my infirmities, that the power of Christ may rest upon me. 2 Corinthians 12:9

- Finally, my brethren, be strong in the Lord and in the power of His might. Ephesians 6:10

- I can do all things through Christ who strengthens me. Philippians 4:13

- But may the God of all grace, who called us to His eternal glory by Christ Jesus, after you have suffered a while, perfect, establish, strengthen, and settle you. 1 Peter 5:10

Thankfulness

- Therefore I will give thanks to You, O Lord, among the Gentiles, And sing praises to Your name. 2 Samuel 22:50

- Oh, give thanks to the Lord! Call upon His name; Make known His deeds among the peoples! 1 Chronicles 16:8

- Oh, give thanks to the Lord, for He is good! For His mercy endures forever. 1 Chronicles 16:34

- That I may proclaim with the voice of thanksgiving, And tell of all Your wondrous works. Psalm 26:7

- Sing praise to the Lord, you saints of His, And give thanks at the remembrance of His holy name. Psalm 30:4

- I will give You thanks in the great assembly; I will praise You among many people. Psalm 35:18

- Offer to God thanksgiving, And pay your vows to the Most High. Psalm 50:14

- I will praise the name of God with a song, And will magnify Him with thanksgiving. Psalm 69:30

- We give thanks to You, O God, we give thanks! For Your wondrous works declare that Your name is near. Psalm 75:1

- So we, Your people and sheep of Your pasture, will give You thanks forever; We will show forth Your praise to all generations. Psalm 79:13

- It is good to give thanks to the Lord, And to sing praises to Your name, O Most High; Psalm 92:1

- Let us come before His presence with thanksgiving; Let us shout joyfully to Him with psalms. Psalm 95:2

- Rejoice in the Lord, you righteous, And give thanks at the remembrance of His holy name. Psalm 97:12

- Enter into His gates with thanksgiving, And into His courts with praise. Be thankful to Him, and bless His name. Psalm 100:4

- Oh, give thanks to the Lord! Call upon His name; Make known His deeds among the peoples! Psalm 105:1

- Praise the Lord! Oh, give thanks to the Lord, for He is good! For His mercy endures forever. Psalm 106:1

- Oh, give thanks to the Lord, for He is good! For His mercy endures forever. Psalm 107:1

- Oh, that men would give thanks to the Lord for His goodness, And for His wonderful works to the children of men! Psalm 107:8

- Let them sacrifice the sacrifices of thanksgiving, And declare His works with rejoicing. Psalm 107:22

- I will offer to You the sacrifice of thanksgiving, And will call upon the name of the Lord. Psalm 116:17

- Oh, give thanks to the Lord, for He is good! For His mercy endures forever. Psalm 118:1

- Sing to the Lord with thanksgiving; Sing praises on the harp to our God, Psalm 147:7

- But thanks be to God, who gives us the victory through our Lord Jesus Christ. 1 Corinthians 15:57

- Thanks be to God for His indescribable gift! 2 Corinthians 9:15

- giving thanks always for all things to God the Father in the name of our Lord Jesus Christ, Ephesians 5:20

- Be anxious for nothing, but in everything by prayer and supplication, with thanksgiving, let your requests be made known to God; Philippians 4:6

- giving thanks to the Father who has qualified us to be partakers of the inheritance of the saints in the light. Colossians 1:12

- And let the peace of God rule in your hearts, to which also you were called in one body; and be thankful. Colossians 3:15

- And whatever you do in word or deed, do all in the name of the Lord Jesus, giving thanks to God the Father through Him. Colossians 3:17

- Continue earnestly in prayer, being vigilant in it with thanksgiving; Colossians 4:2

- Therefore by Him let us continually offer the sacrifice of praise to God, that is, the fruit of our lips, giving thanks to His name. Hebrews 13:5

- saying: "Amen! Blessing and glory and wisdom, Thanksgiving and honor and power and might, Be to our God forever and ever. Amen." Revelation 7:12

- saying: "We give You thanks, O Lord God Almighty, The One who is and who was and who is to come, Because You have taken Your great power and reigned. Revelation 11:17

Words/Tongue

- My lips will speak no evil, and my tongue will speak no lies. Job 27:4 (NLT)

- Those who lead blameless lives and do what is right, speaking the truth from sincere hearts. Psalm 15:2 (NLT)

- Let the words of my mouth and the meditation of my heart Be acceptable in Your sight, O Lord, my strength and my Redeemer. Psalm 19:14

- Then keep your tongue from speaking evil and your lips from telling lies! Psalm 34:13 (NLT)

- The mouth of the righteous speaks wisdom, And his tongue talks of justice. Psalm 37:30

- I said to myself, "I will watch what I do and not sin in what I say. I will hold my tongue when the ungodly are around me." Psalm 39:1 (NLT)

- My mouth shall speak wisdom, And the meditation of my heart shall give understanding. Psalm 49:3

- Let my mouth be filled with Your praise And with Your glory all the day. Psalm 71:8

- My mouth shall tell of Your righteousness And Your salvation all the day, For I do not know their limits. Psalm 71:15

- I will sing of the mercies of the Lord forever; With my mouth will I make known Your faithfulness to all generations. Psalm 89:1

- I will greatly praise the Lord with my mouth; Yes, I will praise Him among the multitude. Psalm 109:30

- Set a guard, O Lord, over my mouth; Keep watch over the door of my lips. Psalm 141:3

- My mouth shall speak the praise of the Lord, And all flesh shall bless His holy name Forever and ever. Psalm 145:21

- Put away from you a deceitful mouth, And put perverse lips far from you. Proverbs 4:24

- A worthless person, a wicked man, Walks with a perverse mouth; Proverbs 6:12

- For my mouth will speak truth; Wickedness is an abomination to my lips. Proverbs 8:7

- All the words of my mouth are with righteousness; Nothing crooked or perverse is in them. Proverbs 8:8

- Too much talk leads to sin. Be sensible and keep your mouth shut. Proverbs 10:19 (NLT)

- The lips of the godly speak helpful words, but the mouth of the wicked speaks perverse words. Proverbs 10:32 (NLT)

- Some people make cutting remarks, but the words of the wise bring healing. Proverbs 12:18 (NLT)

- Truthful words stand the test of time, but lies are soon exposed. Proverbs 12:19 (NLT)

- Those who control their tongue will have a long life; opening your mouth can ruin everything. Proverbs 13:3 (NLT)

- A soft answer turns away wrath, But a harsh word stirs up anger. Proverbs 15:1

- The tongue of the wise makes knowledge appealing, but the mouth of a fool belches out foolishness. Proverbs 15:2 (NLT)

- Gentle words are a tree of life; a deceitful tongue crushes the spirit. Proverbs 15:4 (NLT)

- The heart of the godly thinks carefully before speaking; the mouth of the wicked overflows with evil words. Proverbs 15:8 (NLT)

- The crooked heart will not prosper; the lying tongue tumbles into trouble. Proverbs 17:20 (NLT)

- The tongue can bring death or life; those who love to talk will reap the consequences. Proverbs 18:21 (NLT)

- Watch your tongue and keep your mouth shut, and you will stay out of trouble. Proverbs 21:23 (NLT)

- As surely as a north wind brings rain, so a gossiping tongue causes anger! Proverbs 25:23

- A lying tongue hates its victims, and flattering words cause ruin. Proverbs 26:28

- "My people bend their tongues like bows to shoot out lies. They refuse to stand up for the truth. They only go from bad to worse. They do not know me," says the Lord. Jeremiah 9:3 (NLT)

- And I tell you this, you must give an account on judgment day for every idle word you speak. Matthew 12:36 (NLT)

- It's not what goes into your mouth that defiles you; you are defiled by the words that come out of your mouth." Matthew 15:11 (NLT)

- Don't use foul or abusive language. Let everything you say be good and helpful, so that your words will be an encouragement to those who hear them. Ephesians 4:29 (NLT)

- Get rid of all bitterness, rage, anger, harsh words, and slander, as well as all types of evil behavior. Ephesians 4:31 (NLT)

- Understand this, my dear brothers and sisters: You must all be quick to listen, slow to speak, and slow to get angry. James 1:19 (NLT)

- For the Scriptures say, "If you want to enjoy life and see many happy days, keep your tongue from speaking evil and your lips from telling lies. 1 Peter 3:10 (NLT)

Bible Quiz Questions

EASY

Q: Who created the heavens and the earth?
A: God

Q: Who was the first man?
A: Adam

Q: Who was first woman?
A: Eve (Adam's wife)

Q: Where did Adam and Eve live?
A: the Garden of Eden

Q: What was the first sin?
A: Eve disobeyed God and ate from the tree of the Knowledge of Good and Evil.

Q: What were the names of Adam and Eve's first two sons?
A: Cain, Abel

Q: Who was the first person murdered? Who killed him?
A: Abel. Cain.

Q: What did God tell Noah to build?
A: An ark

Q: How many of each animal did God tell Noah bring on the ark?
A: 2

Q: How many days did God cause it to rain on the earth?
A: 40 days and 40 nights

Q: What is the symbol of God's promise to Noah?
A: A rainbow

Q: What was the name of the tower the people built where God confused them with different languages?
A: Babel

Q: Who was Abraham's nephew?
A: Lot

Q: What was the name of Abraham's wife?
A: Sarah

Q: Who was Abraham's first son?
A: Ishmael

Q: What did Sarah do when the angel told Abraham she would have a son?
A: Sarah laughed

Q: Who was the son of Abraham and Sarah?
A: Isaac

Q: What happened to Lot's wife when she disobeyed God and looked back?
A: She was turned into a pillar of salt

Q: What did God ask Abraham to do with his son, Isaac?
A: Offer him as a sacrifice.

Q: Who was Isaac's wife?
A: Rebekah

Q: How many children did Isaac have? What were their names?
A: 2: Jacob and Esau (twins)

Q: What did Esau sell for food?
A: His birthright

Q: Who tricked their father into giving them a blessing?
A: Jacob

Q: How many sons did Jacob have?
A: 12

Q: Who was Jacob tricked into marrying?
A: Leah

Q: Who did Jacob work another seven years to marry?
A: Rachel

Q: Who was given a coat of many colors by Jacob?
A: Joseph (his son)

Q: Who was the baby that was put in a basket in the river?
A: Moses

Q: Who found baby Moses in the river?
A: Pharaoh's daughter

Q: What did Moses see in the wildernes that God spoke to him from?
A: Burning bush

Q: What did God tell Moses to tell Pharaoh?
A: "Let My people go."

Q: How did the Israelites get past the Red Sea?
A: God parted the water so they could walk on dry land.

Q: How many years were the Israelites wandering in the wilderness?
A: 40

Q: What did God give to Moses on Mount Sinai?
A: 10 Commandments

Q: What was the name of Moses' brother?
A: Aaron

Q: How many tribes did Israel have?
A: 12

Q: What special food from heaven did God give the Israelites in the wilderness?
A: Manna

Q: What animal spoke to Balaam?
A: Donkey

Q: Which town's walls fell when the Israelites marched around it?
A: Jericho

Q: What strong man had long hair?
A: Samson

Q: Who had Samson's hair cut off, which caused him to lose his strength?
A: Delilah

Q: What prophet of God was taken to heaven in a chariot of fire?
A: Elijah

Q: What child heard God calling to him in the temple?
A: Samuel

Q: Who was the first king of Israel?
A: Saul

Q: People look on the outward appearance, but what does God look on?
A: The heart

Q: What young boy defeated a giant?
A: David

Q: Who was David's best friend?
A: Jonathan

Q: What did King Solomon ask God for?
A: Wisdom

Q: What three Hebrew boys were thrown into a fiery furnace for not bowing to the king's image?
A: Shadrach, Meshach, and Abednego

Q: Who was thrown into a lions' den because he prayed to God three times a day?
A: Daniel

Q: Which prophet was swallowed by a fish?
A: Jonah

Q: What was the name of Jesus's mother?
A: Mary

Q: What did Jesus's earthly father do for a job?
A: He was a carpenter.

Q: What gifts did the wise men bring to Jesus after He was born?
A: Gold, frankincense, and myrrh

Q: What did Jesus use to feed 5,000 people?
A: 5 loaves and 2 fish

Q: How many disciples did Jesus choose?
A: 12

Q: Who had a coat made of camel hair and ate locusts and wild honey?
A: John the Baptist

Q: What was the first miracle of Jesus recorded in the Bible?
A: Turning water into wine

Q: Who baptized Jesus?
A: John

Q: Where was Jesus tempted by Satan?
A: The wilderness

Q: Who appeared with Jesus on the Mount of Transfiguration?
A: Moses and Elijah

Q: Which of the disciples betrayed Jesus?
A: Judas Iscariot

Q: How did Judas identity Jesus to the soldiers?
A: With a kiss

Q: When did Jesus rise from the dead?
A: On the third day

Q: What was another name for the Apostle Paul?
A: Saul of Tarsus

Q: What happened when Paul and Silas were singing in jail?
A: God caused an earthquake and set them free

DIFFICULT:

Q: What was the first thing that God created?
A: Light

Q: On which day did God create plants?
A: Third

Q: What was the name of the first man who didn't die?
A: Enoch; God took him

Q: What man lived the longest on the earth?
A: Methuselah—969 years

Q: Who lived in Ur, and moved to a country he did not know because God told him to?
A: Abraham

Q: Name three sons of Jacob.
A: Reuben, Simeon, Levi, Judah, Dan, Naphtali, Gad, Asher, Issachar, Zebulun, Joseph, and Benjamin.

Q: What was another name for Jacob?
A: Israel

Q: Name one of the ten plagues of Egypt?
A: (1) Water turned to blood, (2) frogs, (3) gnats, (4) flies, (5) livestock disease, (6) boils, (7) hail, (8) locusts, (9) darkness, (10) death of firstborn

Q: What did Samson use to kill 1000 men?
A: A donkey's jawbone

Q: What did Samson tie torches to?
A: Foxes' tails

Q: Name the first three Israelite kings.
A: Saul, David, Solomon

Q: How many years of famine did Joseph tell Pharaoh Egypt would have?
A: 7

Q: What was Jacob's youngest son's name?
A: Benjamin

Q: Which two birds did Noah send out of the ark?
A: Raven and dove

Q: Which commander had leprosy?
A: Naaman

Q: Which towns were destroyed by fire and brimstone?
A: Sodom and Gomorrah

Q: How many people were saved on the ark?
A: 8: Noah, his wife, Shem, his wife, Ham, his wife, Japheth, his wife

Q: What did God use Joseph to do?
A: Interpret dreams, save the Israelite people

Q: What was Samuel's mother's name?
A: Hannah

Q: Was Goliath a Philistine or an Egyptian?
A: Philistine

Q: What are we told to do in the fifth commandment?
A: Honor your father and mother

Q: What was the name of Naomi's daughter-in-law who stayed with her?
A: Ruth

Q: Who married Ruth?
A: Boaz

Q: Who was the first woman to judge Israel?
A: Deborah

Q: Who asked God to have the sun and moon to stand still for one day?
A: Joshua

Q: How many books are in the Bible?
A: 66

Q: How many books are in the Old Testament?
A: 39

Q: How many books are in the New Testament?
A: 27

Q: What four books tell about Jesus's life on Earth?
A: Matthew, Mark, Luke, and John

Q: What king ordered all baby boys under the age of two killed?
A: Herod

Q: Where did Jesus grow up?
A: Nazareth

Q: What was the name of the sea where Jesus calmed a storm?
A: The Sea of Galilee

Q: What are the only two angels named in the Bible?
A: Michael and Gabriel

Q: What is the first book in the Bible?
A: Genesis

Q: What is the last book in the Bible?
A: Revelation

Q: What is the longest book in the Bible?
A: Psalms

Q: What is the shortest book in the Bible?
A: 3 John

Bible Board Games

- ♠ Cranium Bible Edition Game
- ♠ Bible Sequence Game
- ♠ Bible Trivia Board Game
- ♠ Children's Bible Trivia Board Game
- ♠ Bible-opoly Game
- ♠ Scrabble: Bible Edition
- ♠ Bible Mad Gab
- ♠ Outburst!: Bible Edition
- ♠ Scattergories: Bible Edition
- ♠ Bible Challenge Game
- ♠ Bible Taboo
- ♠ Bible BLURT!
- ♠ Bible TriBond
- ♠ Bible Pictionary
- ♠ Apples to Apples: Bible Edition
- ♠ The American Bible Challenge Board Game
- ♠ Guesstures: Bible Edition

Bible Movies/TV Shows

- **The Book of Daniel**
  DVD PURE FLIX ENTERTAINMENT, LLC, 2013

- **Amazing Love: The Story of Hosea**
  DVD BMG

- **One Night with the King**
  DVD FOX FAITH

- **The Nativity Story**
  DVD WARNER HOME VIDEO

- **The Bible: The Epic MiniSeries**
  DVD FOX FAITH, 2013

- **A.D. The Bible Continues**
  DVD FOX FAITH, 2015

- **The Visual Bible: Matthew**
  RANDOLF PRODUCTIONS INC

Books of the Bible

I feel it is important to know all the books of the Bible in their order. This helps you to find scripture verses easier and faster! There are many ways to learn them. There are many children's songs available that teach the books of the bible. Here are just a few:

- ♫ "Bible Book Bop" **Go Fish**
- ♫ "Wonderful Books of the Bible" **Craig Anderson**
- ♫ "Books of the Bible" **Rebecca Lou**
- ♫ "The Books of the Bible Song" **Bert Cross II**
- ♫ "Wonderful Books of the Bible" **Jill Anderson**
- ♫ "Books of the Bible" **Alan W. Lemke**
- ♫ "Bible Train Express" **Lumin8 Children's Choir**

Parents, you can also give your kids a fill-in-the-blank "test" on the books of the Bible. I think the **Sword Drills** are also a great way to see if your family is learning them!

The following pages have the books of the Bible listed for you, grouped by Old and New Testaments.

39 Books of the Old Testament:

1. Genesis
2. Exodus
3. Leviticus
4. Numbers
5. Deuteronomy
6. Joshua
7. Judges
8. Ruth
9. 1 Samuel
10. 2 Samuel
11. 1 Kings
12. 2 Kings
13. 1 Chronicles
14. 2 Chronicles
15. Ezra
16. Nehemiah
17. Esther
18. Job
19. Psalms
20. Proverbs
21. Ecclesiastes
22. Song of Solomon
23. Isaiah
24. Jeremiah
25. Lamentations
26. Ezekiel
27. Daniel
28. Hosea
29. Joel
30. Amos
31. Obadiah
32. Jonah
33. Micah
34. Nahum
35. Habakkuk
36. Zephaniah
37. Haggai
38. Zechariah
39. Malachi

27 Books in New Testament:

1. Matthew
2. Mark
3. Luke
4. John
5. Acts
6. Romans
7. 1 Corinthians
8. 2 Corinthians
9. Galatians
10. Ephesians
11. Philippians
12. Colossians
13. 1 Thessalonians
14. 2 Thessalonians
15. 1 Timothy
16. 2 Timothy
17. Titus
18. Philemon
19. Hebrews
20. James
21. 1 Peter
22. 2 Peter
23. 1 John
24. 2 John
25. 3 John
26. Jude
27. Revelation

Notes

We want to hear from YOU!

How are you implementing
the ideas from
The Scripture Life at Home?

Do you have any other
creative ways
to place God's Word
into your daily life?

Please share with us!
You can contact us at

www.thescripturelife.com!

We will also have the latest updates
on materials that will help you
live God's Word!

Be a part of
The Scripture Life
today...and EVERYDAY!

Made in the USA
Lexington, KY
27 July 2018